contents

behind

Where is Marmaduke?

He is hiding behind
a vase of flowers.
Can you see him
peeping out?

in front

Hello, Marmaduke!

Marmaduke is sitting in front of the vase of flowers.

Now you can see all of me.

up

Marmaduke is climbing up the slide.

I feel a bit scared up here.

down

Marmaduke slides down to the bottom.

I feel much safer down here!

on

Marmaduke is pretending to be in a circus. He is balancing on a ball.

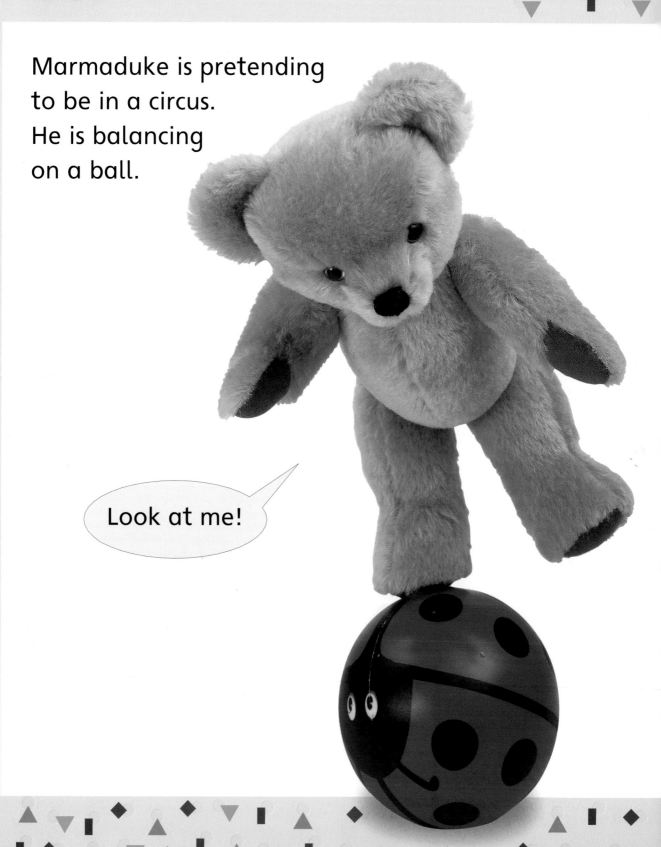

off

Oh dear!
Marmaduke has fallen off the ball.

Ouch!

in

Marmaduke is sitting
in a bucket.
What a funny place
to sit!

Marmaduke is getting out of the bucket.

That bucket was not very comfortable!

over

Marmaduke is feeling sporty. He is jumping over a rope.

This is quite difficult!

under

Marmaduke has thought of something different to try. Now he is crawling under the rope.

This is much easier!

inside

Can you spot Marmaduke?
He is hiding inside the box.
You can just see his eyes and his nose.

outside

Now Marmaduke is outside the box.

It was dark inside the box but it is light outside the box.

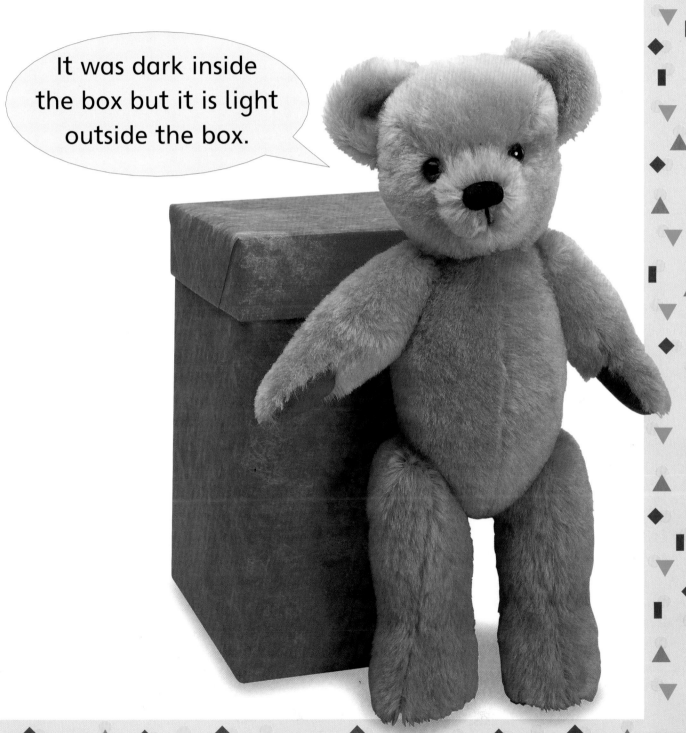

above

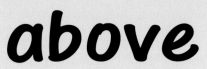

Marmaduke is standing above a car.

If I look down, I can see the car.

below

Marmaduke is standing below a ball.

I have to look up to see the ball.

17

beside

Marmaduke is standing beside his basket of building blocks.

The blocks are next to me.

through

Marmaduke has built an archway with his blocks. He is walking through the archway.

I am walking from one side to the other.

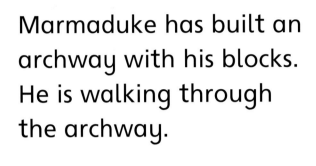

between

Marmaduke is sitting between
two toy cars.

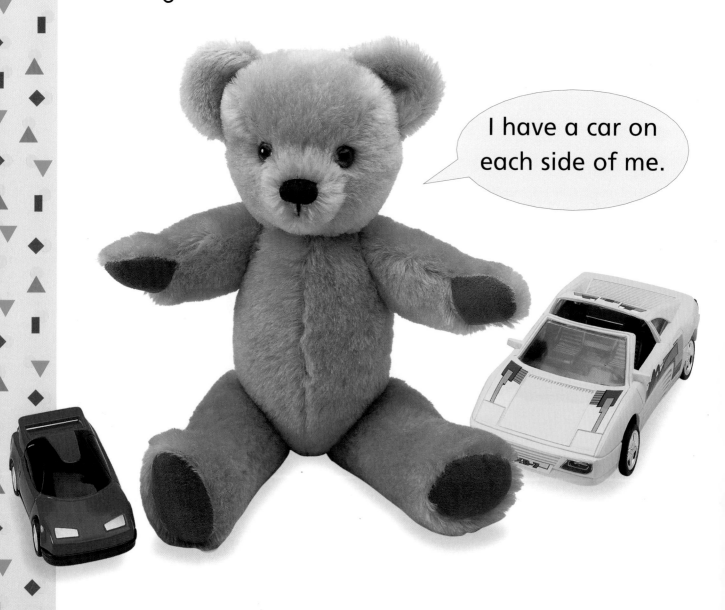

I have a car on
each side of me.

among

Marmaduke is playing with all his cars.
He is sitting among the cars.

Where is Marmaduke?

Marmaduke can use different words to describe where he is sitting.

I am sitting on a bucket, between two watering cans.

glossary

archway a doorway shape that people or objects can go through

balancing staying on something wobbly without falling off

describe say where something or someone is

peeping looking out from behind something

pretending acting as though you are something or someone else

index

24